JUST BRICK IT

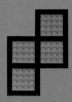

Author, Model Maker and Designer:
David Scarfe

Editor: Lucienne O'Mara
Photographer: Andy Pickford
Cover designer: Ana Bjezancevic

First published in Great Britain in 2015 by LOM ART, an imprint of
Michael O'Mara Books Limited, 9 Lion Yard, Tremadoc Road, London SW4 7NQ

W www.mombooks.com
f Michael O'Mara Books
y @OMaraBooks

A CIP catalogue record for this book is available from the British Library.

ISBN: 978-1-910552-02-5

2 4 6 8 10 9 7 5 3

Printed and bound in China

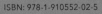

INTRODUCTION

We all loved building with bricks when we were young, but why stop? This book is for the big kids who still want to play.

Whether you brighten up your car with some LEGO® dice or make a set of floppy disk coasters for your friend, these projects are enjoyable to construct and will bring a little nostalgic cool to your home.

Both practical and retro, the designs rate from quick and easy builds to some that are more satisfyingly challenging for the more experienced AFOL.

From a red-hot flaming toast rack to a wall-mounted deer head, there's plenty to try. Let's Brick It!

RATING

HARD ------------------

MEDIUM ------------------

EASY ------------------

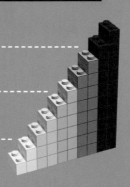

CONTENTS

A 1980s arcade classic turned handy stationery holder – what could be better? Save your desk from an invasion of clutter and add a little nostalgia to your working day.

5x	4x	4x
2x	4x	6x
8x	2x	2x
6x	7x	4x
2x	6x	8x
14x	15x	8x
4x	3x	24x
4x	16x	2x
4x	3x	4x
12x	2x	8x
1x		
1x		

BLUE INVADER

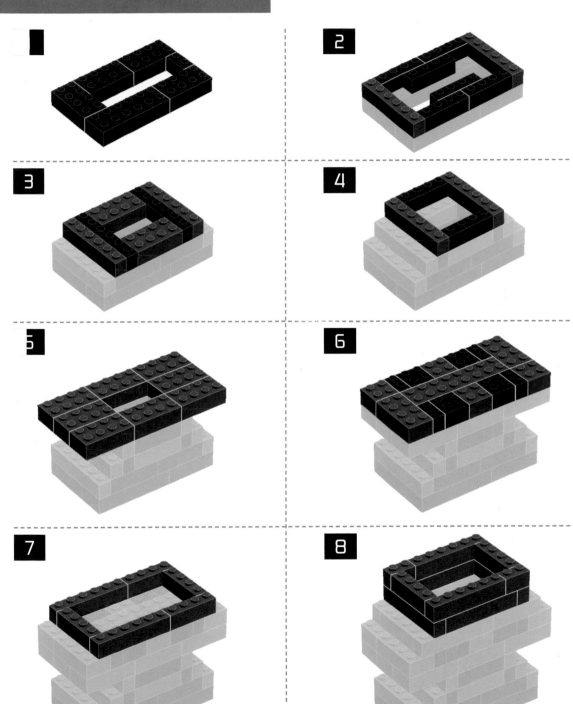

YELLOW INVADER

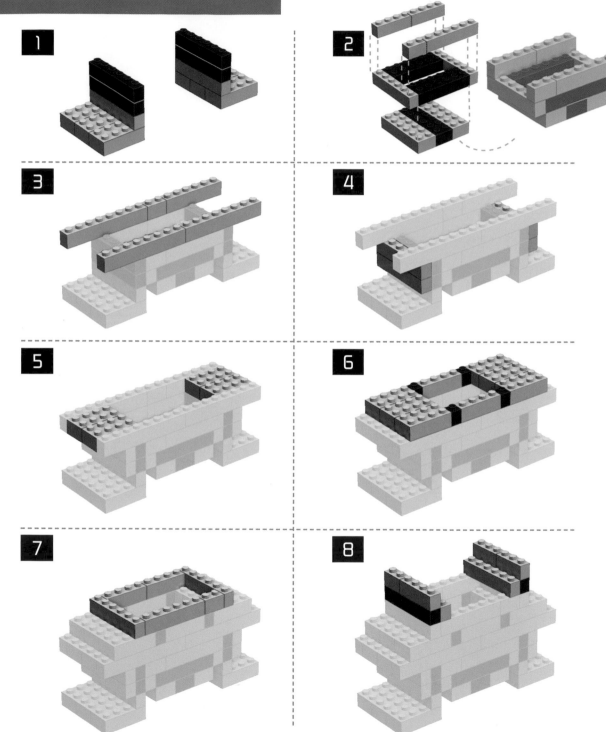

RED INVADER

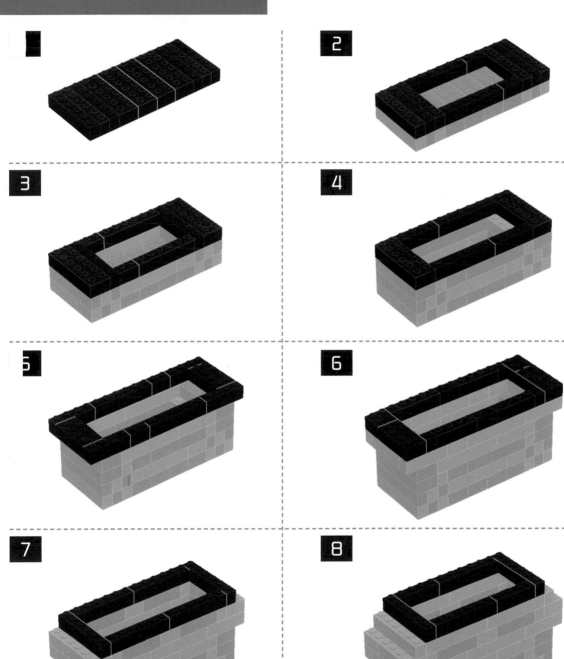

CURSOR BOOK ENDS

I THINK, THEREFORE I AM

A CLASSICAL EDUCATION

I WANDERED LONELY AS A CLOUD…

AN APPLE A DAY

I BEFORE E (EXCEPT AFTER C)

I USED TO KNOW THAT

REMEMBER, REMEMBER (THE FIFTH OF NOVEMBER)

SPILLING THE BEANS ON THE CAT'S PYJAMAS

I USED TO KNOW THAT: ENGLISH

I USED TO KNOW THAT: MATHS

Sick of waiting for a web page to load? Tired of pointing and clicking all day? Turn your frustration into a set of book ends that fill your home with a bit of cyber cool.

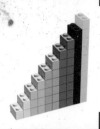

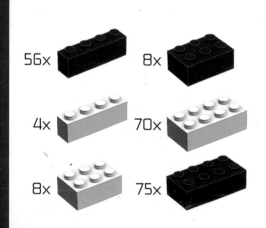

56x 8x

4x 70x

8x 75x

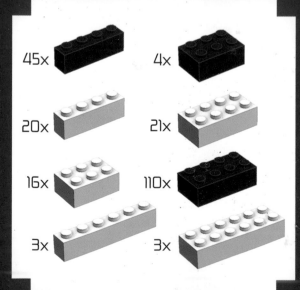

45x 4x

20x 21x

16x 110x

3x 3x

EACH BASE

1

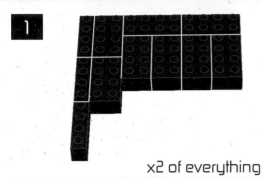

x2 of everything

2

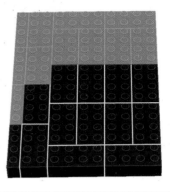

3

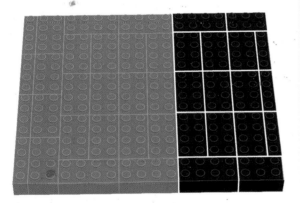

4

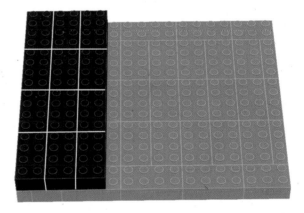

5

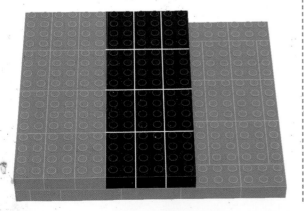

6

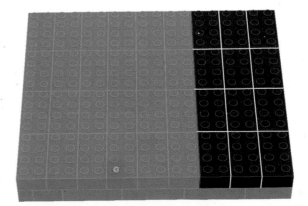

CURSOR

1

2

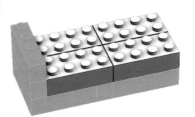

3

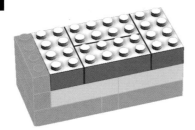

4

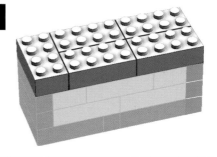

5

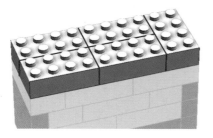

6

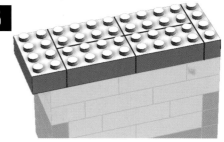

7

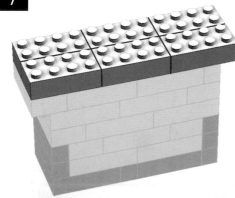

8

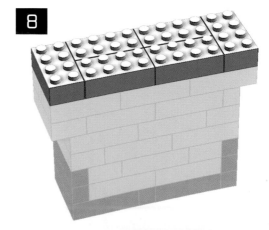

9

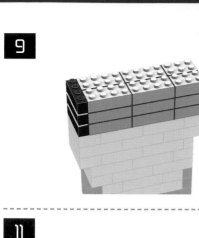

10

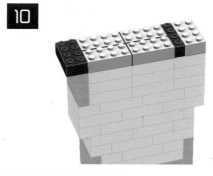

11

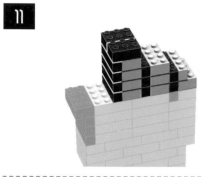

12

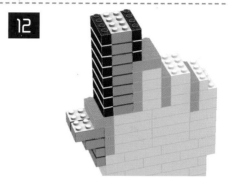

13

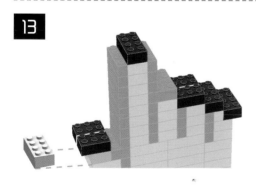

15

14

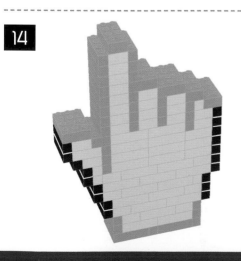

HOUR GLASS

1

2

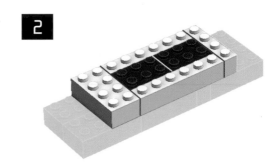

3

4

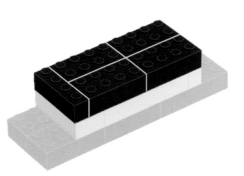

5

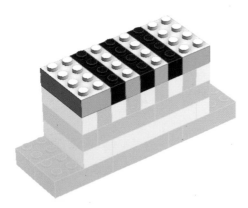

6

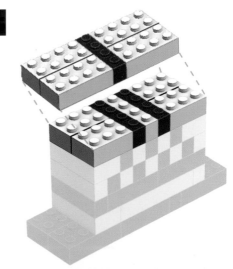

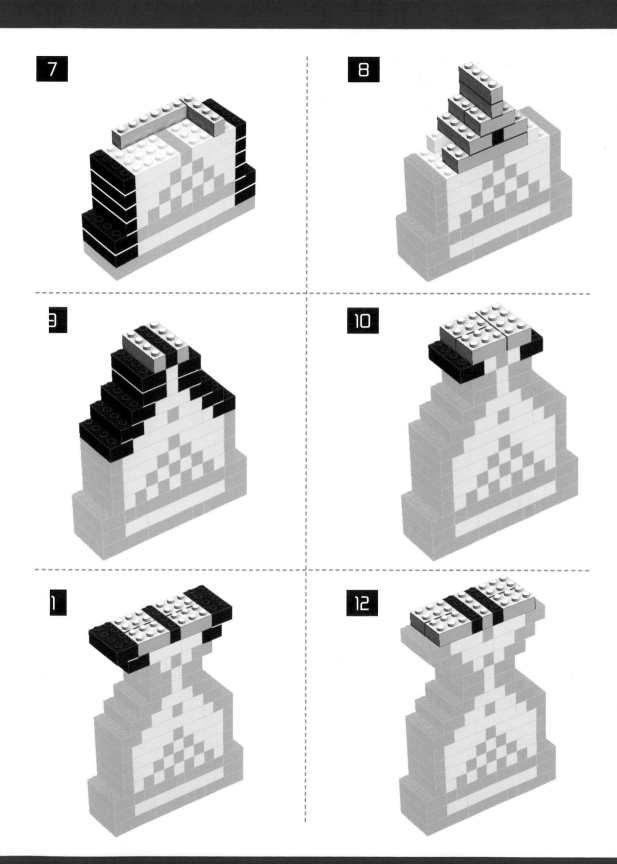

13

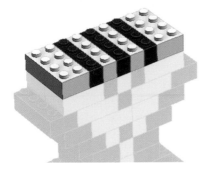

14

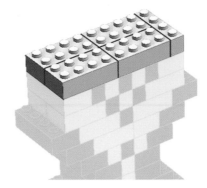

15

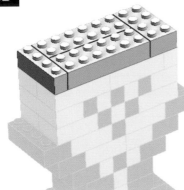

16

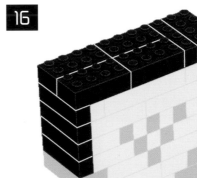

17

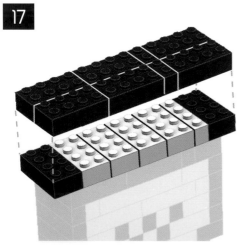

18

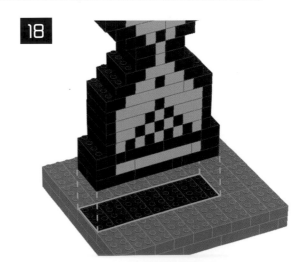

RUBBER DUCK

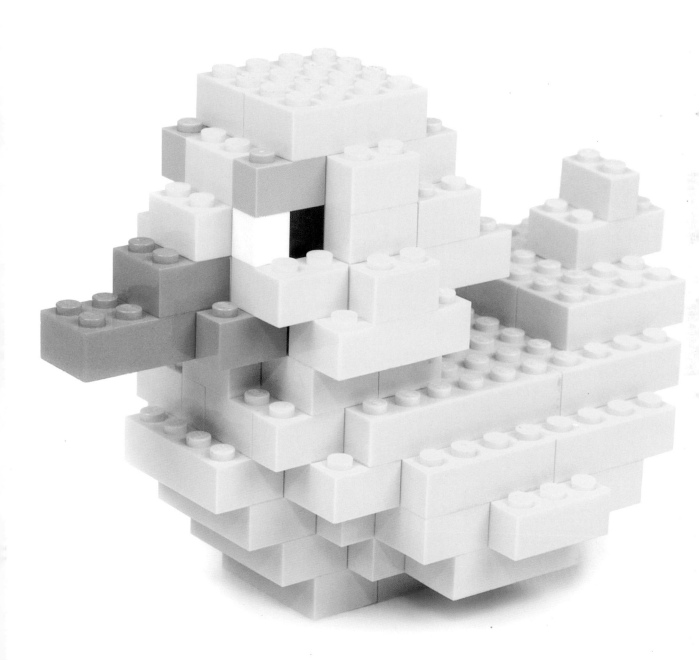

A perfect addition to bath time, this rubber ducky will take you back to those childhood bath times after a long, hard day. Just watch out where he goes – some of those corners are a little sharp. Ouch!

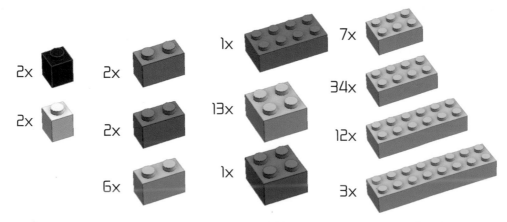

2x

2x

2x

2x

6x

1x

13x

1x

7x

34x

12x

3x

THE HEAD

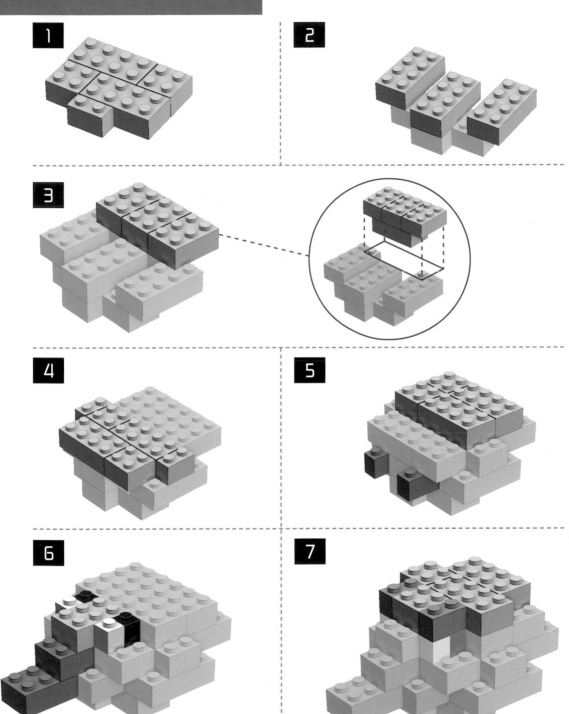

8

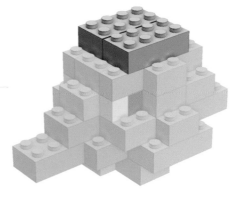

1

2

3

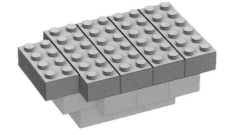

4

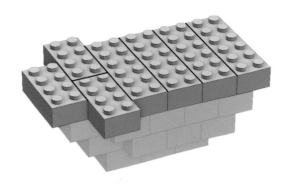

5

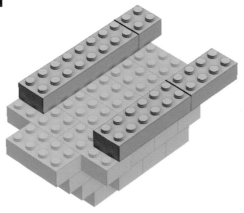

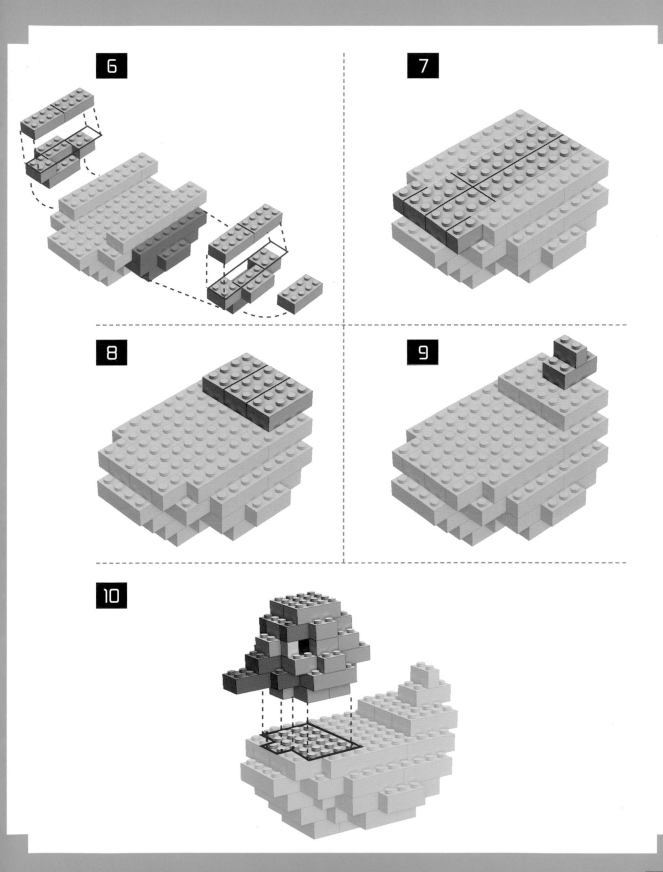

FLYING DUCKS

Time to bring these back into fashion. Ideal for any home in need of a little 1960s charm. Don't forget to add a lava lamp and beaded curtain for full effect.

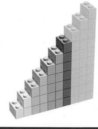

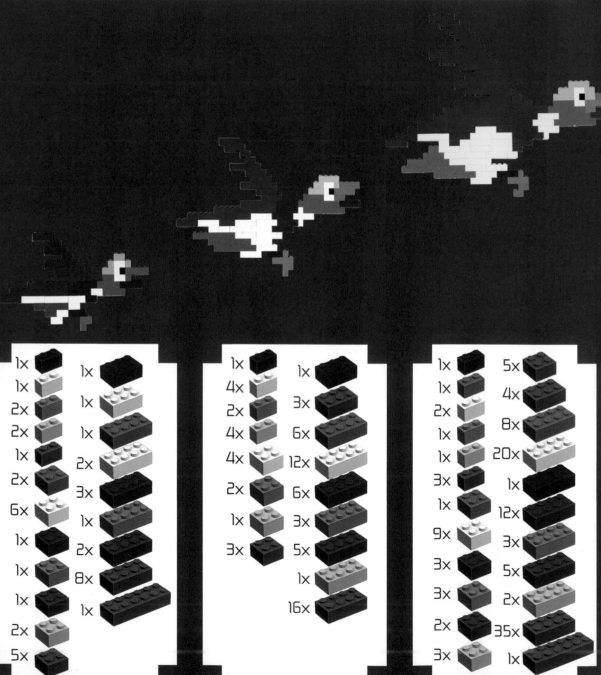

SMALL DUCK

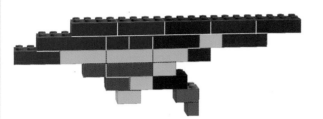

MEDIUM DUCK

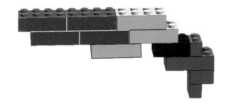

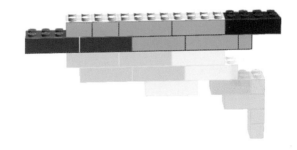

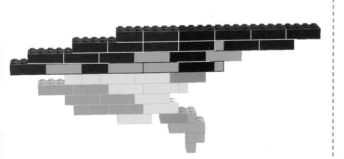

LARGE DUCK

1

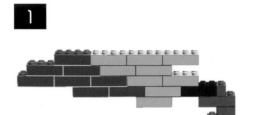

2

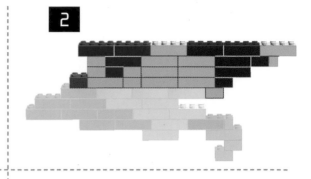

3

4

5

6

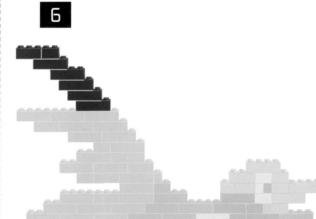

Give your tree a personal touch with these Santa and snowman decorations. Easy to make, they are a perfectly pixelated addition to any Christmas.

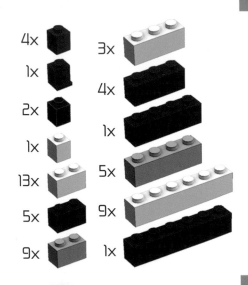

4x
1x
2x
1x
13x
5x
9x
3x
4x
1x
5x
9x
1x

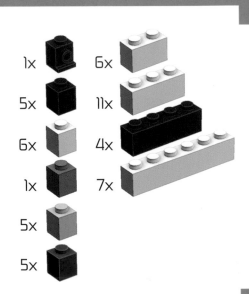

1x
5x
6x
1x
5x
5x
6x
11x
4x
7x

SANTA

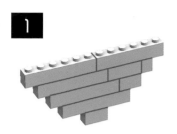

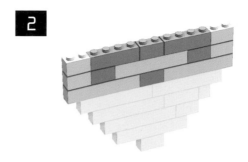

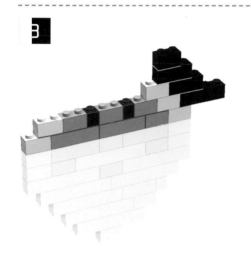

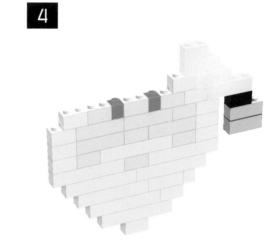

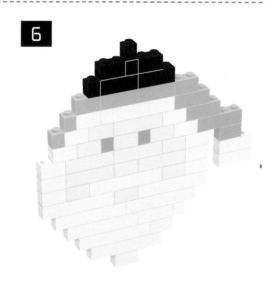

SNOWMAN

1

2

3

4

5

6

Keep your toast nice and warm with this flaming-hot rack. Just watch your fingers!

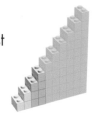

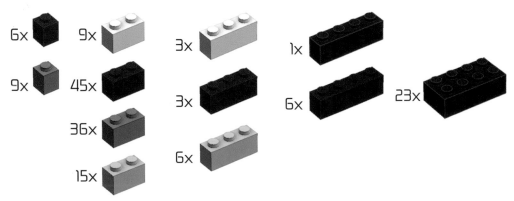

6x   9x   3x   1x

9x   45x   3x   6x   23x

36x

15x   6x

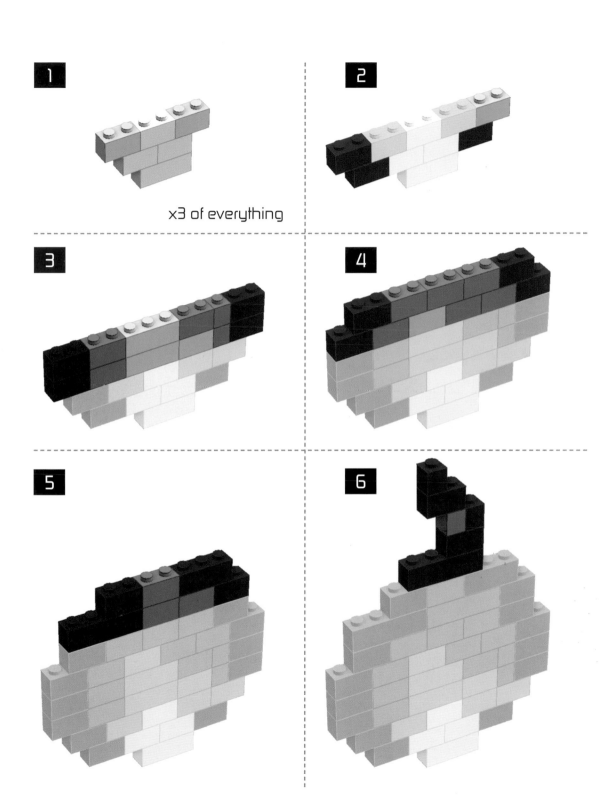

x3 of everything

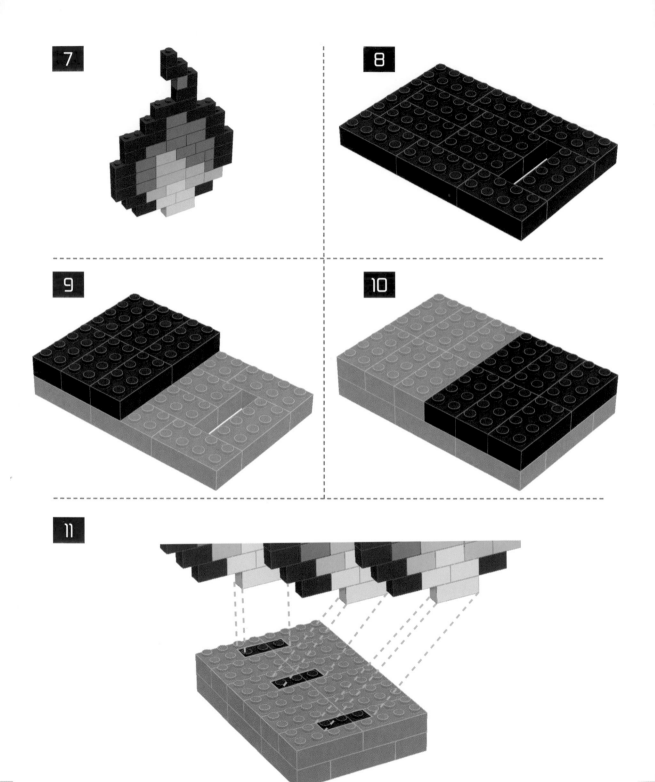

BRAIIIIINNNSSS! Where better to store your pencils than poked into the brain of a reanimated human corpse? Be the envy of your friends with your own Night of the Living Lead.

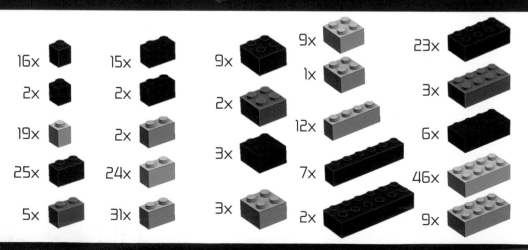

16x   15x   9x   9x   23x

2x   2x   1x   3x

19x   2x   2x   12x   6x

25x   24x   3x   7x   46x

5x   31x   3x   2x   9x

1

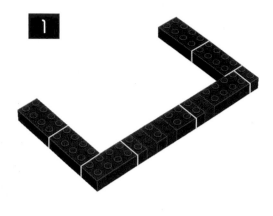

2

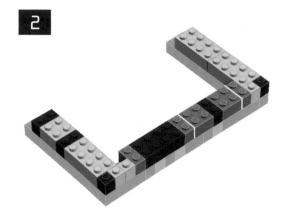

3

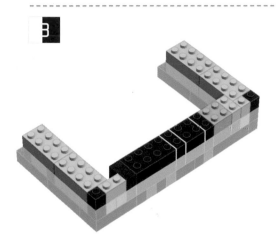

4

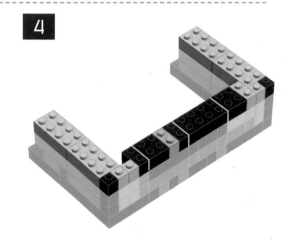

5

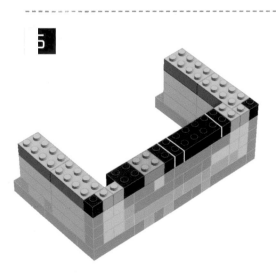

6

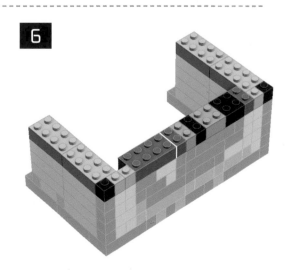

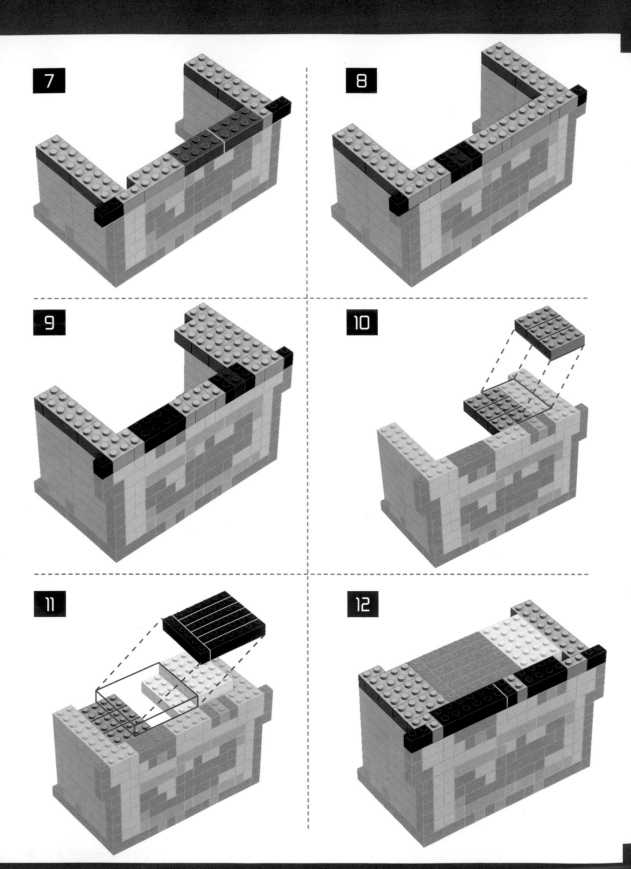

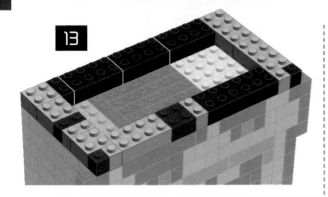

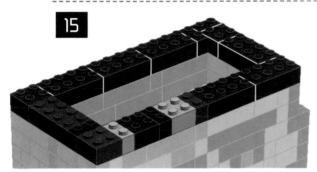

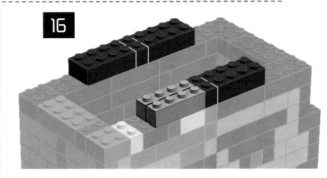

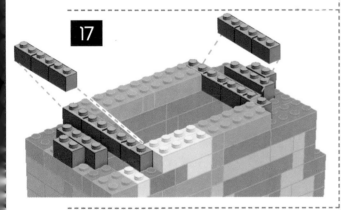

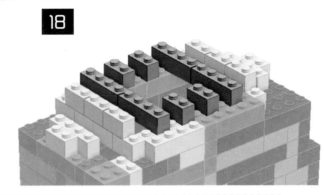

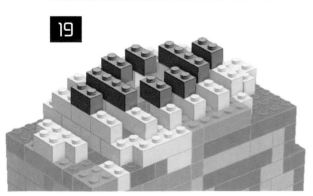

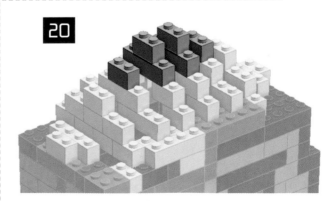

We all have friends whose dinner parties should come with warnings. Why not massively offend them by making a gift of these HAZMAT mats?

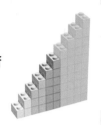

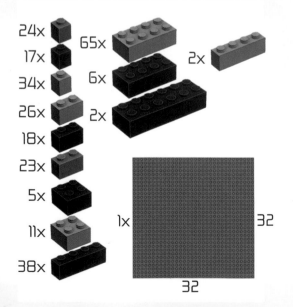

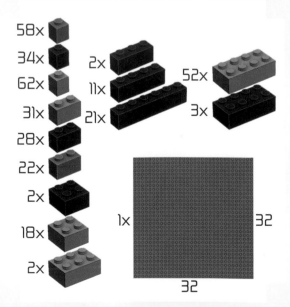

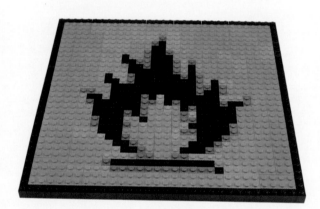

24x
17x
34x
26x
18x
23x
5x
11x
38x

65x
6x
2x

2x

1x   32

32

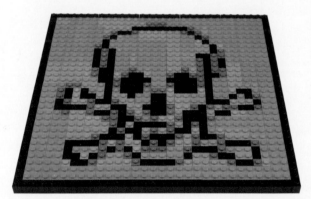

58x
34x
62x
31x
28x
22x
2x
18x
2x

2x
11x
21x

52x
3x

1x   32

32

FLAMMABLE MAT

1

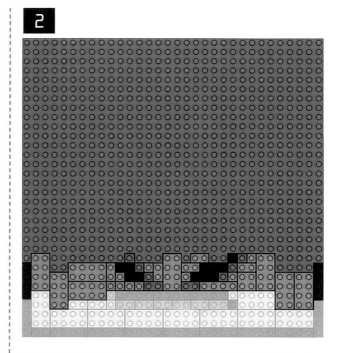

2

3

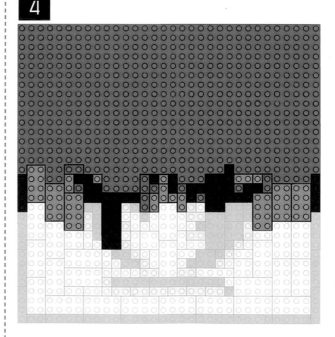

4

5

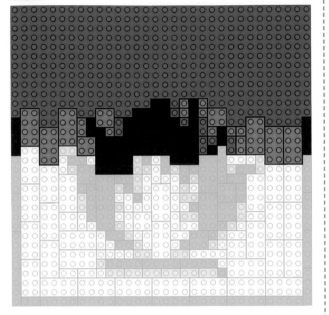

6

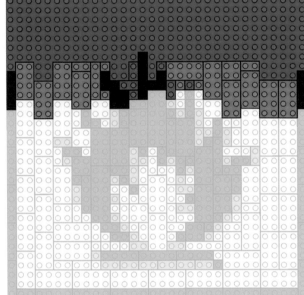

7

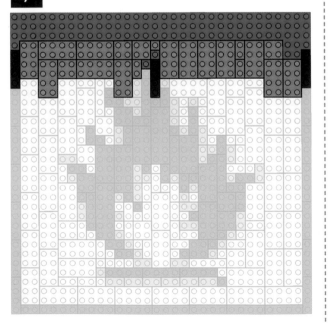

8

TOXIC MAT

1

2

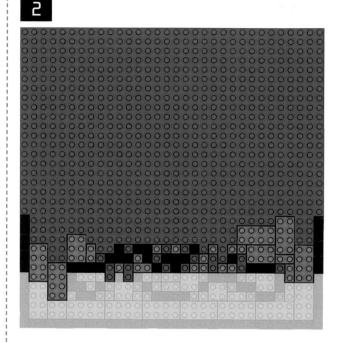

3

4

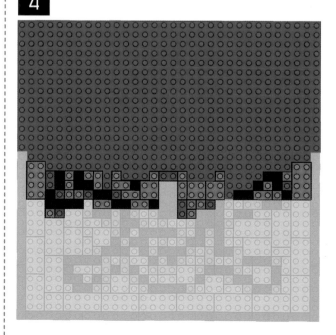

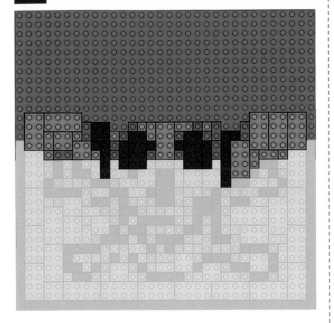

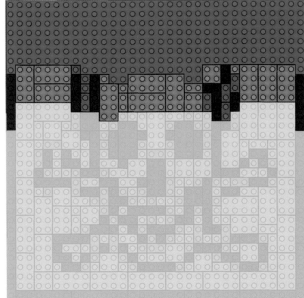

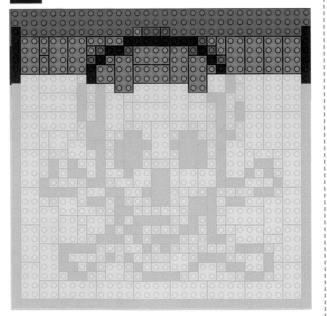

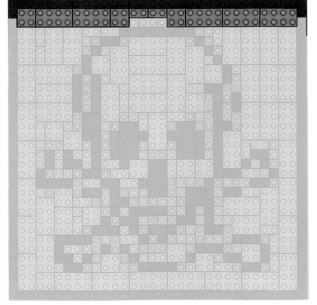

HANGING GHOST

Impress your friends at Halloween with this hanging decoration. More cute than scary, it's the perfect party piece to inject a little humour into the horror.

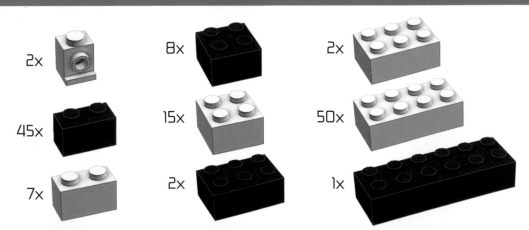

2x

8x

2x

45x

15x

50x

7x

2x

1x

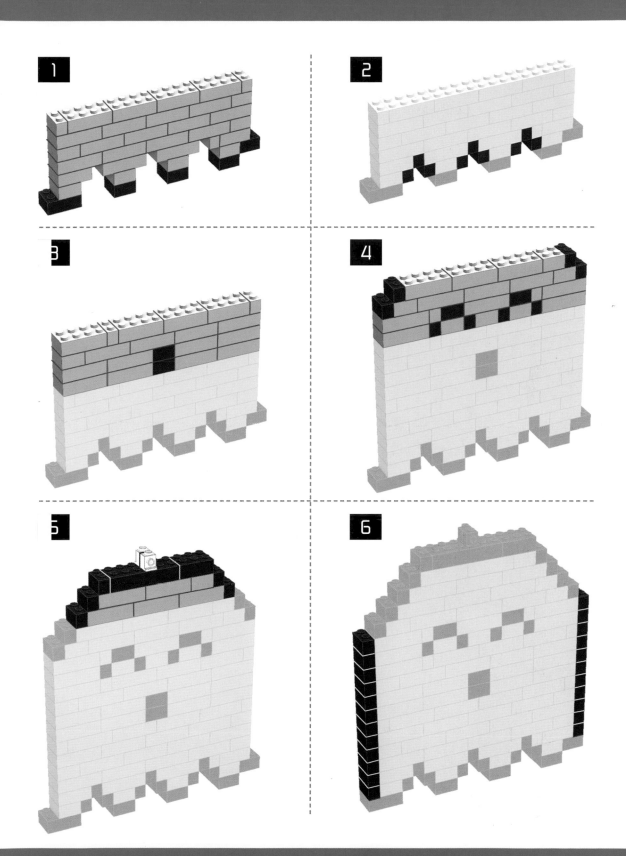

FLOPPY DISK COASTERS

Who says floppy disks serve no purpose? Set down your mug and enjoy a byte of lunch with this geeky favourite.

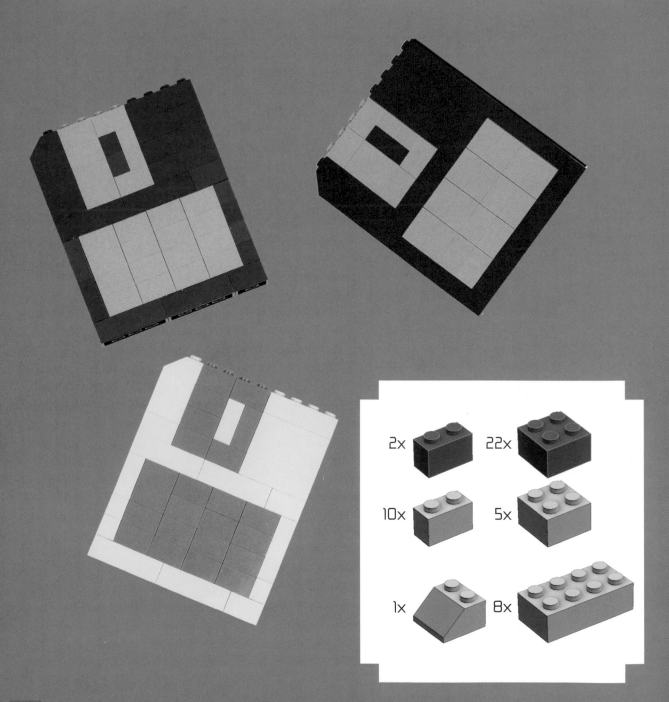

2x

22x

10x

5x

1x

8x

1

2

3

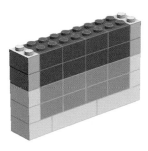

4

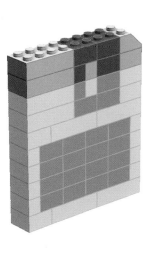

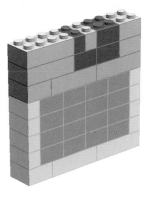

CASSETTE LETTER HOLDER

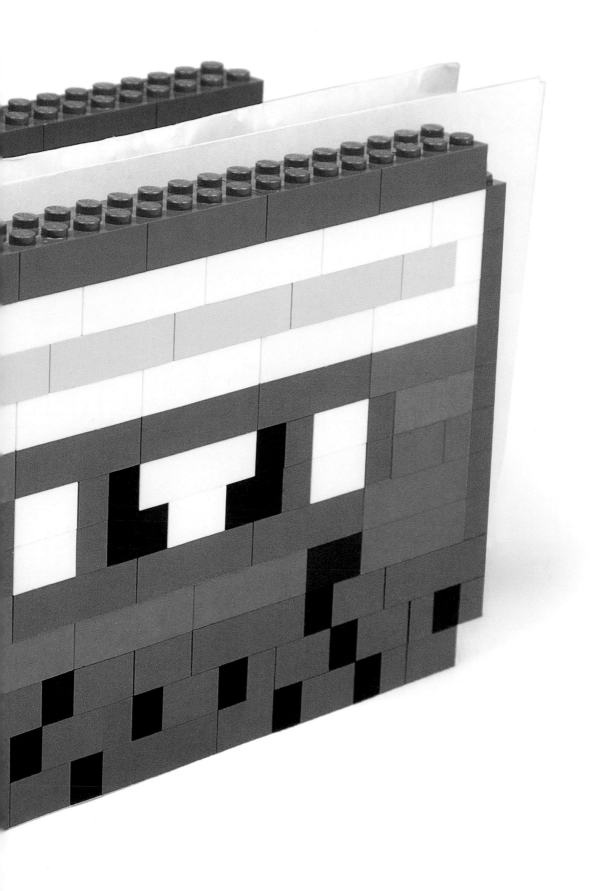

You've heard of a CD rack, but this is oh so much better. Why not give your desk space a vintage twist with this audio classic?

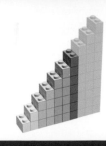

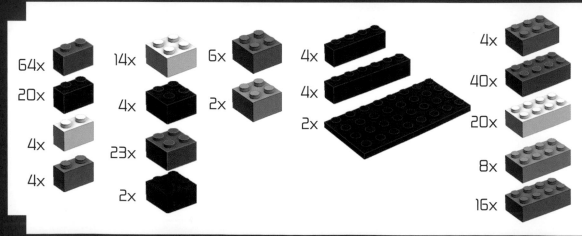

64x
20x
4x
4x

14x
4x
23x
2x

6x
2x

4x
4x
2x

4x
40x
20x
8x
16x

THE BASE

1

2

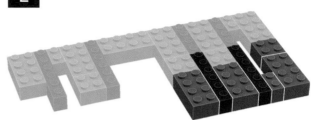

3

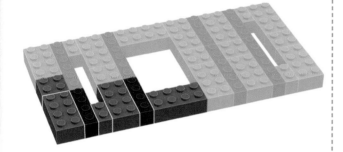

4

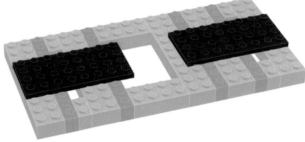

THE TAPES

1

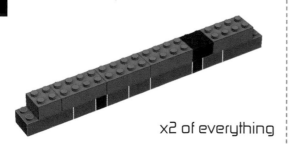

x2 of everything

2

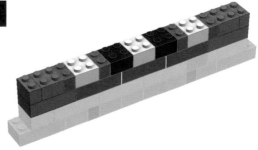

3

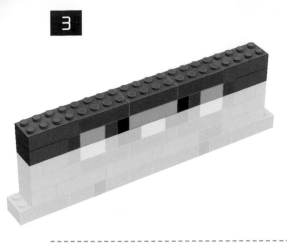

4

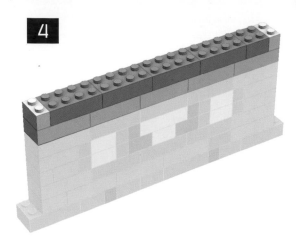

5

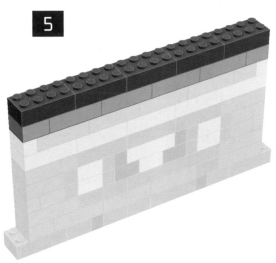

6

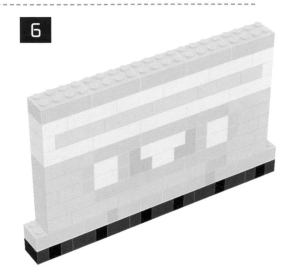

7

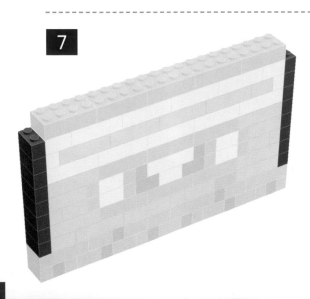

8

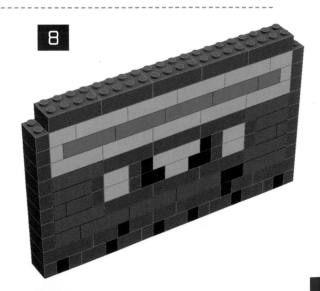

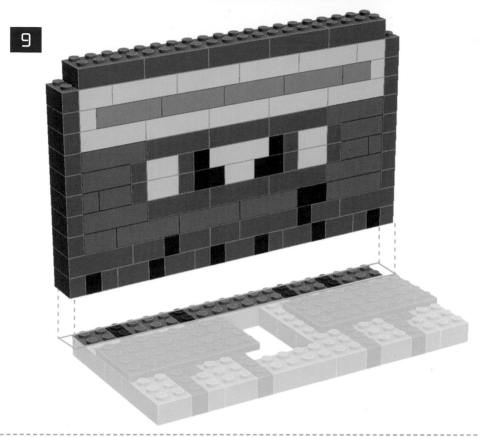

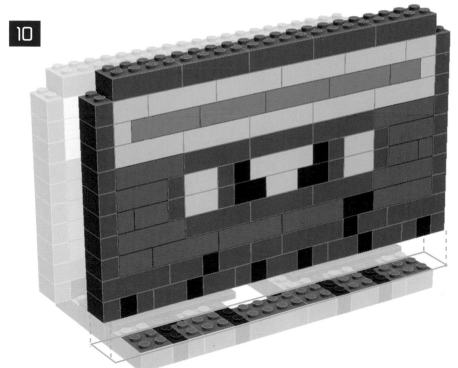

SWORD-IN-THE-STONE PAPERWEIGHT

Prove yourself to be the one true king with this medieval masterpiece, which, when built, will safeguard all your important documents.

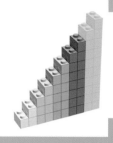

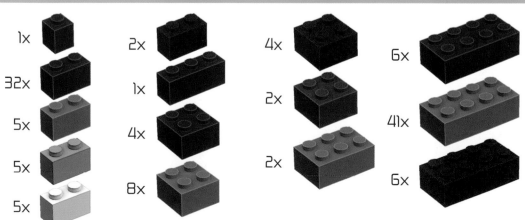

1x

32x

5x

5x

5x

2x

1x

4x

8x

4x

2x

2x

6x

41x

6x

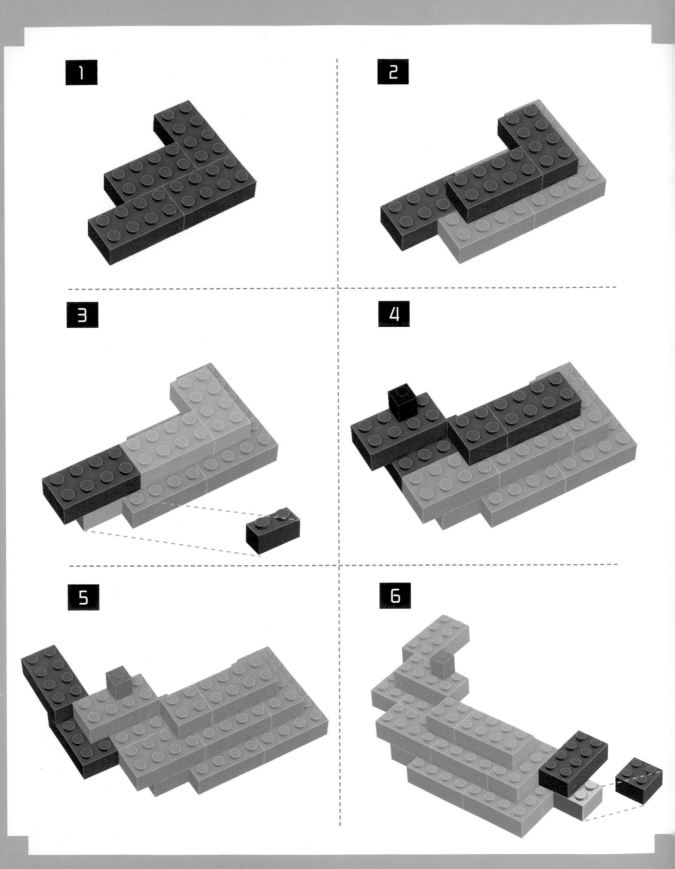

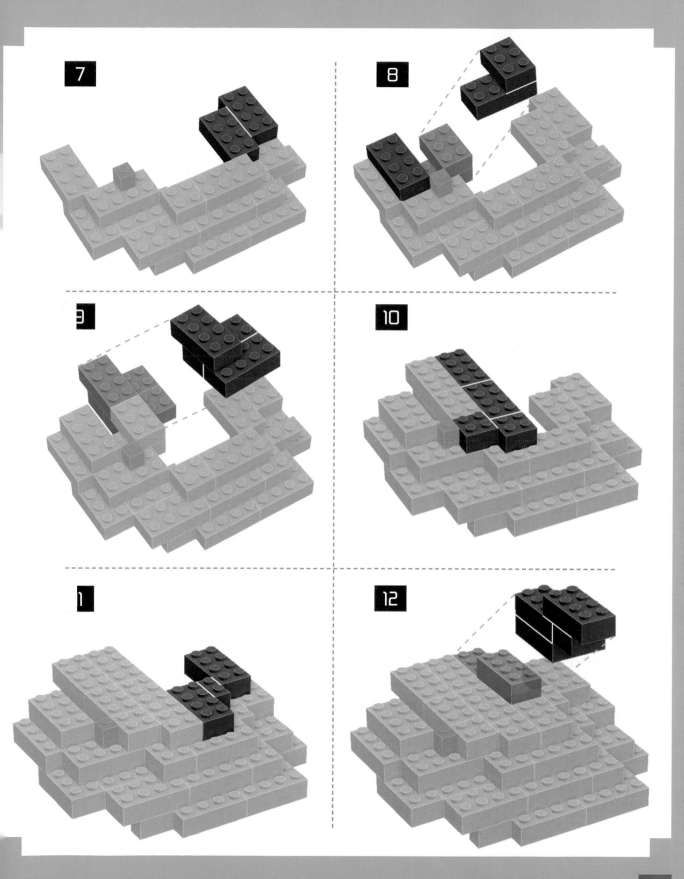

13

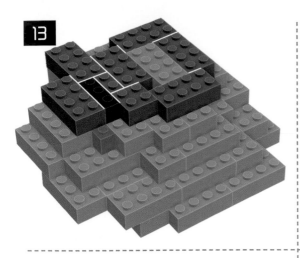

14

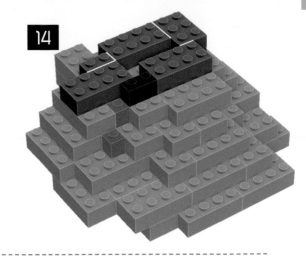

15

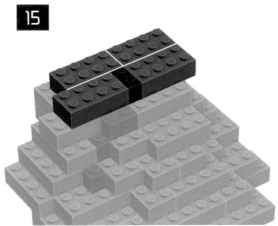

16

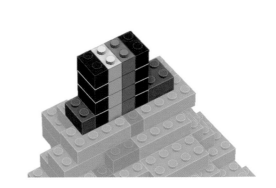

17

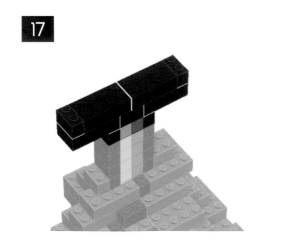

18

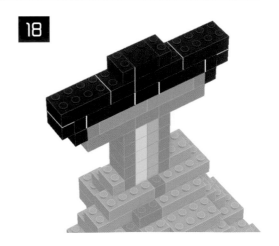

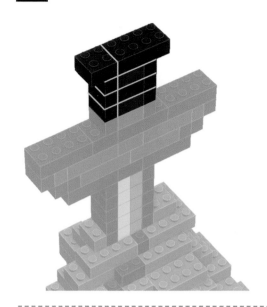

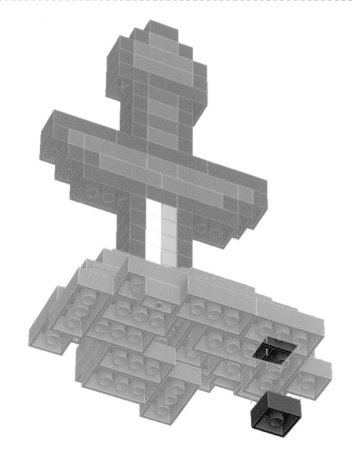

RETRO CONTROLLER PHONE STATION

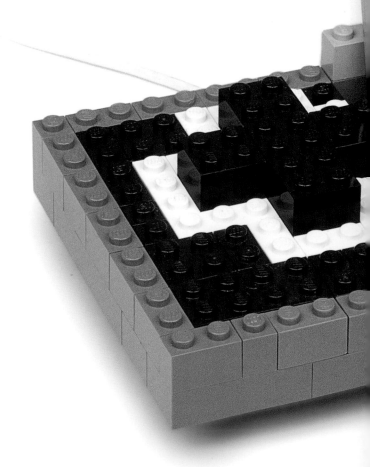

Tap into some misty-eyed nostalgia with this retro controller. Not only a stylish place to leave your phone, but a salute to your inner gamer.

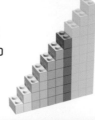

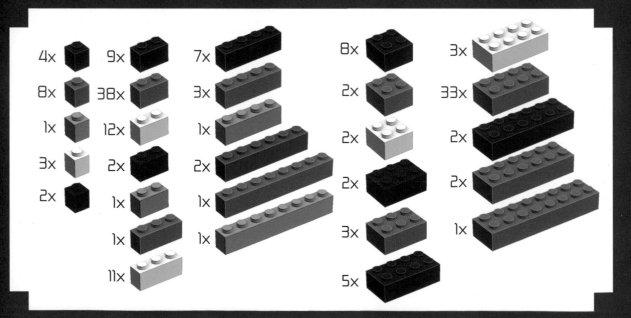

4x   9x   7x   8x   3x

8x   38x   3x   2x   33x

1x   12x   1x   2x

3x   2x   2x   3x   2x

2x   1x   1x   2x

1x   1x   1x

11x   5x

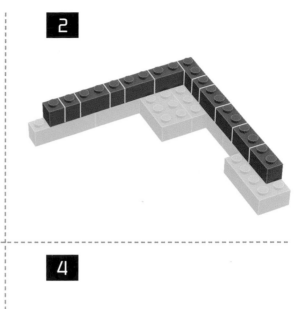

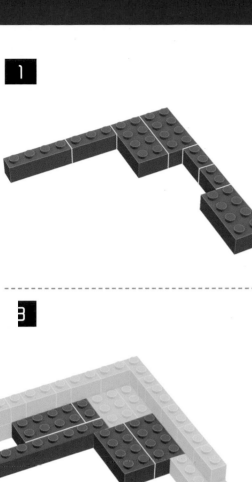

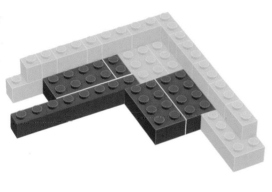

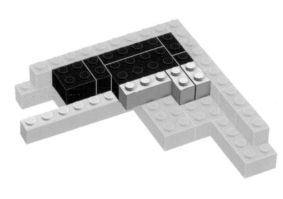

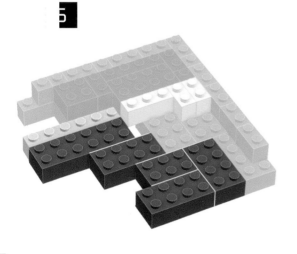

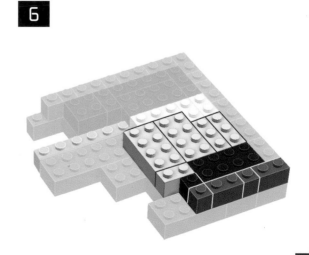

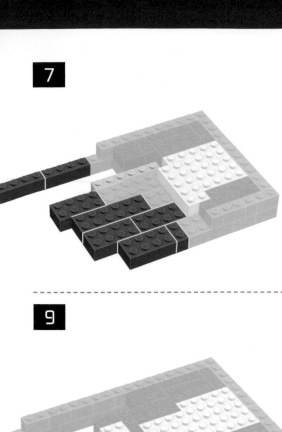

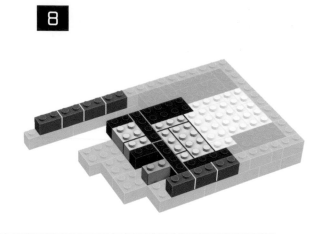

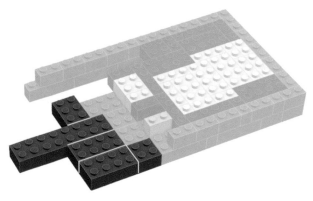

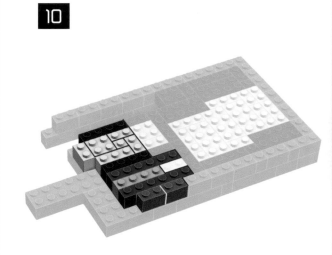

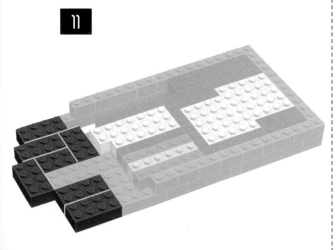

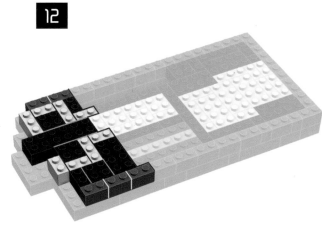

13

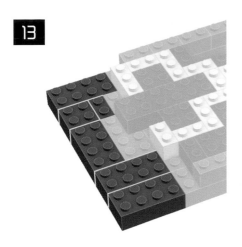

14

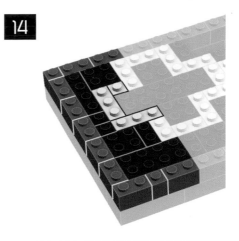

5

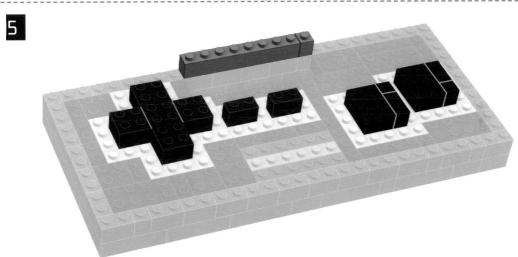

6

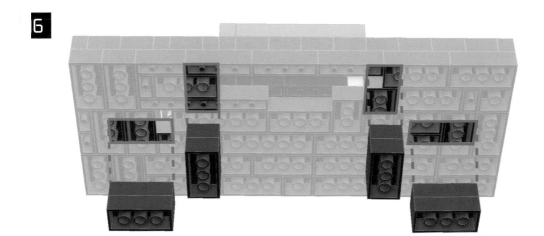

LADY LIBERTY FISH TANK

It's time to revisit the *Planet of the Apes*. Give yourself a constant reminder of the dangers of our simian brothers taking over with this filmic fish-tank scene.

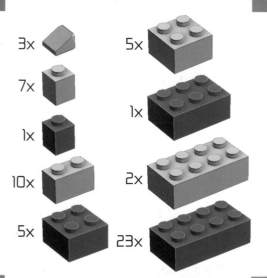

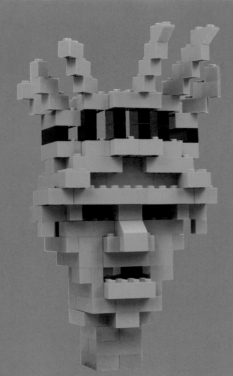

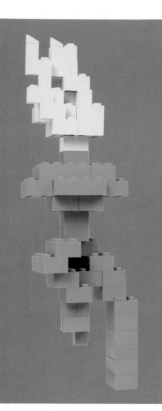

3x

7x

1x

10x

5x

5x

1x

2x

23x

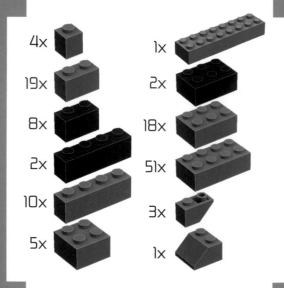

4x

19x

8x

2x

10x

5x

1x

2x

18x

51x

3x

1x

THE HEAD

1

2

3
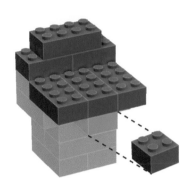

4

5
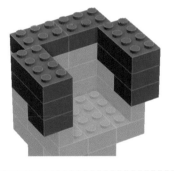

6
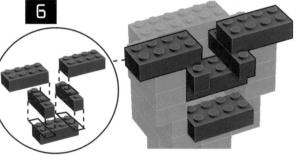

7
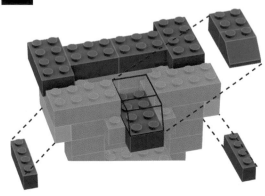

8
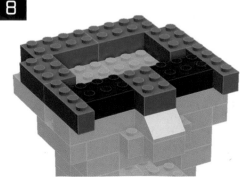

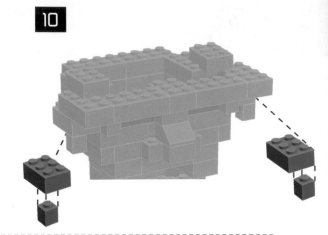

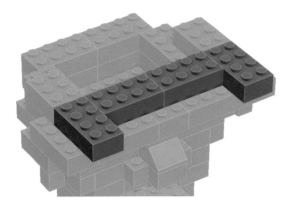

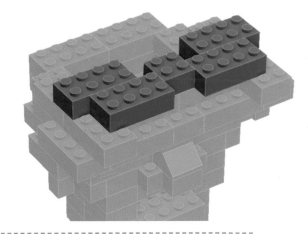

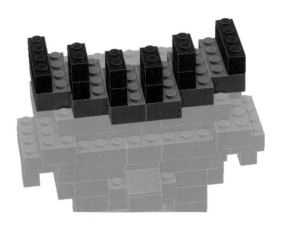

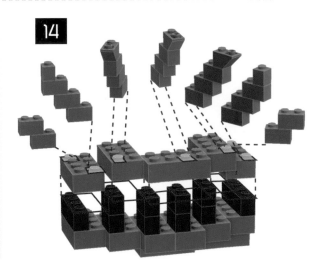

THE TORCH

1

2

3

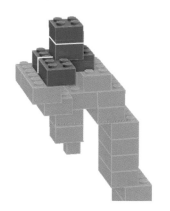

4

5

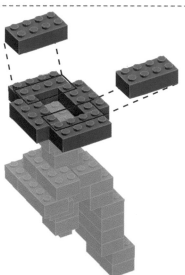

6

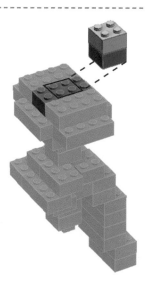

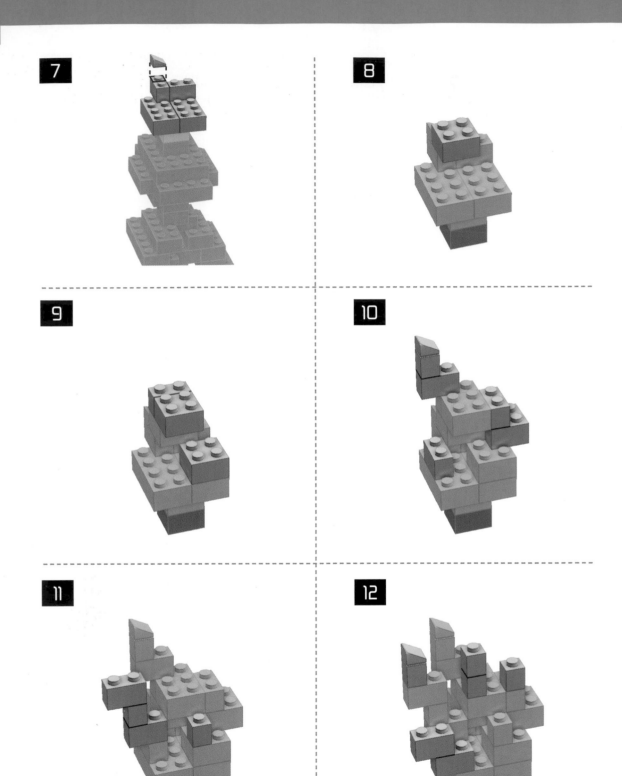

See page 128 for display instruction

HANGING DICE

An update to the 1950s classic, hang these in your car and be the envy of everyone else on the road. That's just how you roll . . .

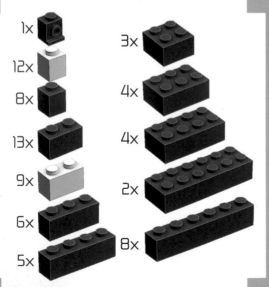

1x
12x
8x
13x
9x
6x
5x

3x
4x
4x
2x
8x

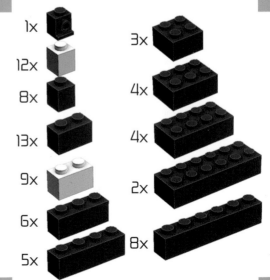

1x
12x
8x
13x
9x
6x
5x

3x
4x
4x
2x
8x

1

2

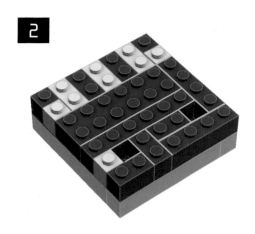

3

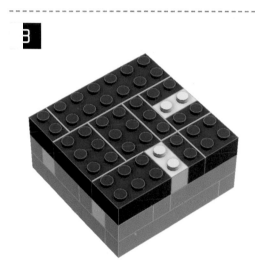

4

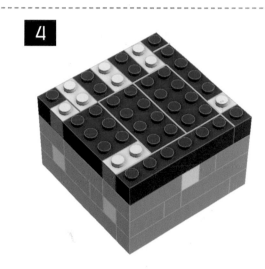

5

6

Repeat in red

If you're sick of losing things, then this could be the key to your problems. Once assembled, the five handy hooks are the safest place to leave your keys.

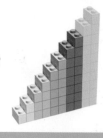

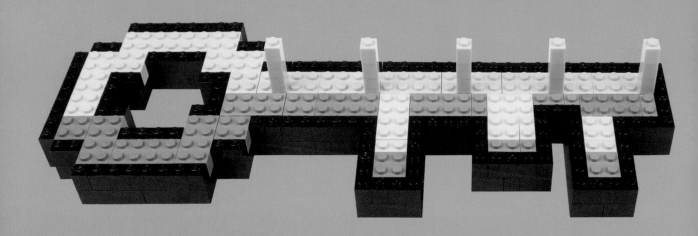

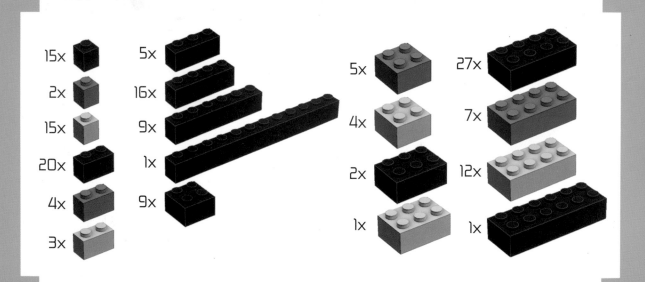

15x
2x
15x
20x
4x
3x

5x
16x
9x
1x
9x

5x
4x
2x
1x

27x
7x
12x
1x

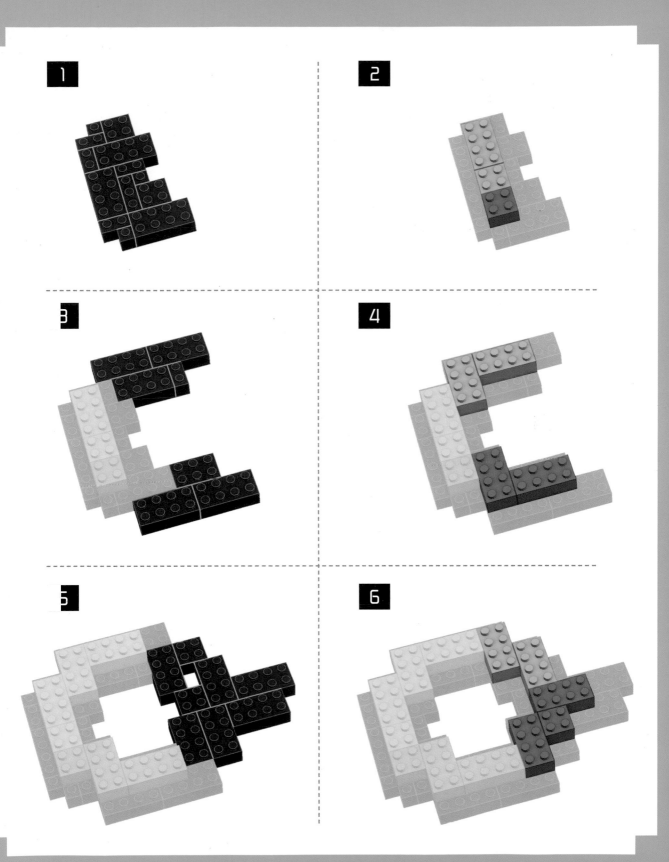

7

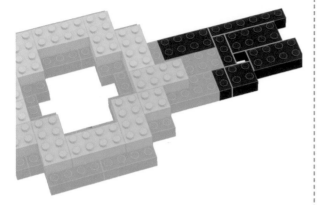

8

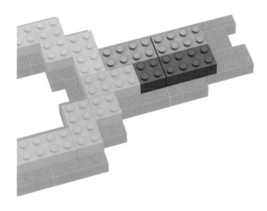

9

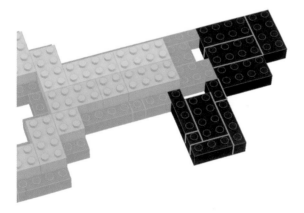

10

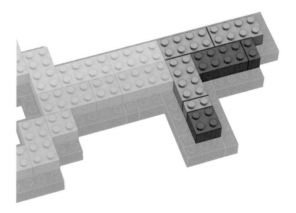

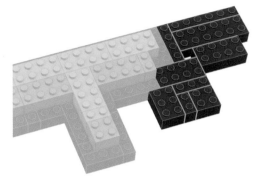

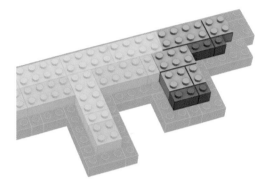

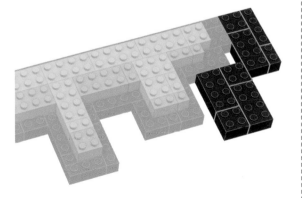

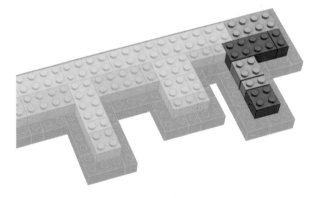

All the thrill of the hunt without any of the blood. Give your home that mountain cabin feel with this bricky trophy. Tricky to construct, but once built, hang it on your wall and proudly display your status as a LEGO® master.

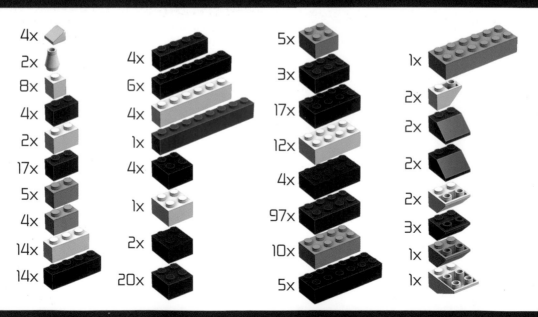

4x

2x

8x

4x

2x

17x

5x

4x

14x

14x

4x

6x

4x

1x

4x

1x

2x

20x

5x

3x

17x

12x

4x

97x

10x

5x

1x

2x

2x

2x

2x

3x

1x

1x

1

2

3

Reverse view

5

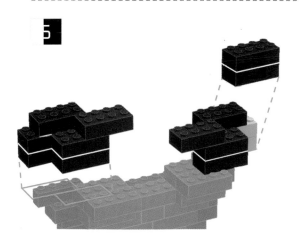

6

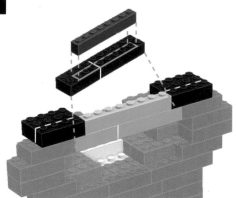

Reverse view

7

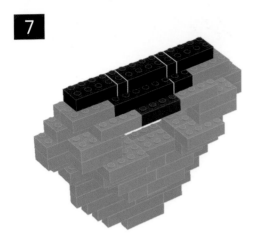

8

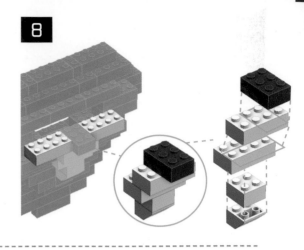

9

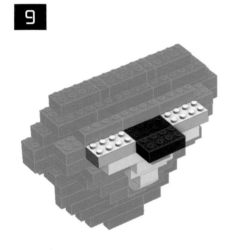

10

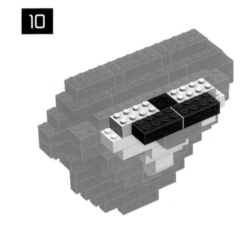

11

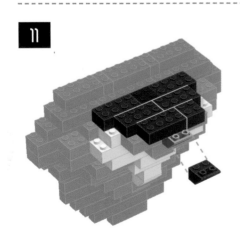

12

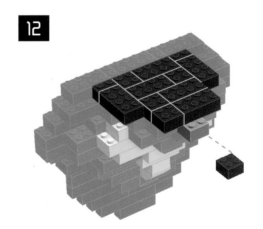

13

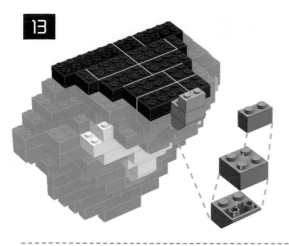

14

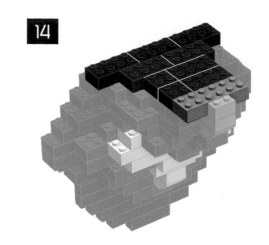

5

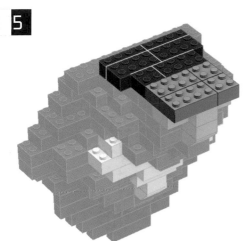

16

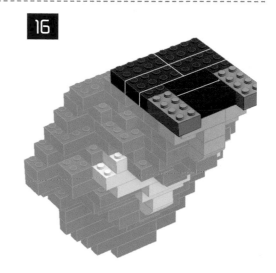

7

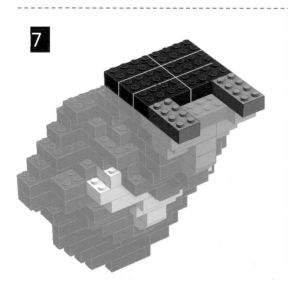

18

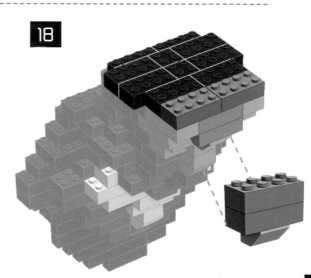

19

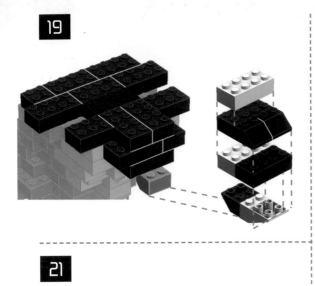

20

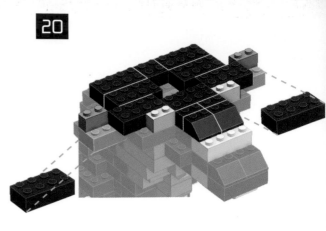

21

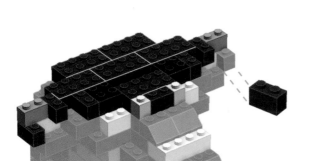

22

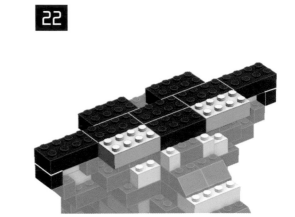

23

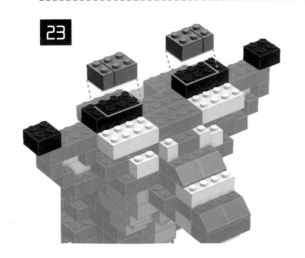

24

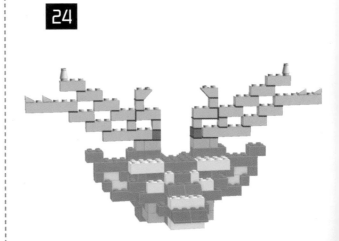

See page 128 for hanging instruction

Missing the best game of all time? Then bring back memories of this vintage classic. Your fridge has never looked so good.

4x

6x

1x

2x

7x

2x

1x

13x

8x

1x

1x

9x

6x

1x

12x

8x

2x

2x

6x

6x

1x

13x

8x

2x

1x

12x

6x

12x

8x

2x

1x

9x

7x

1x

1x

12x

8x

RED BRICKS

1

2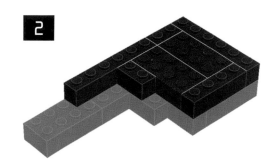

3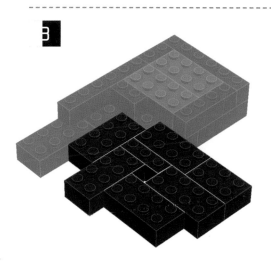

4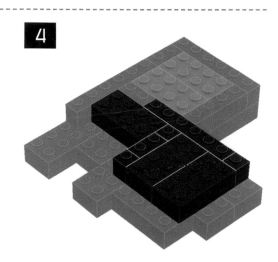

5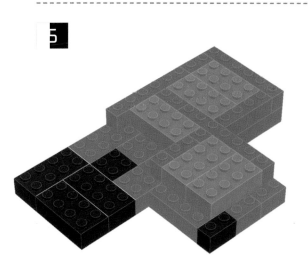

6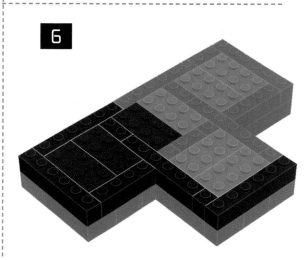

YELLOW BRICKS

1
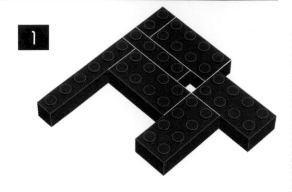

2
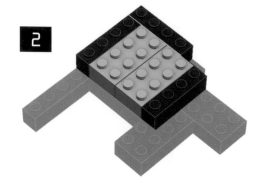

3
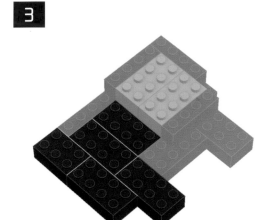

4
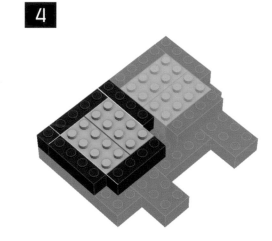

5
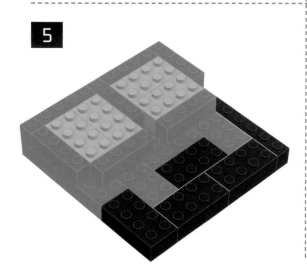

6
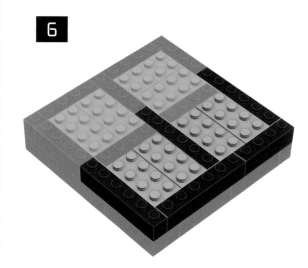

ORANGE BRICKS

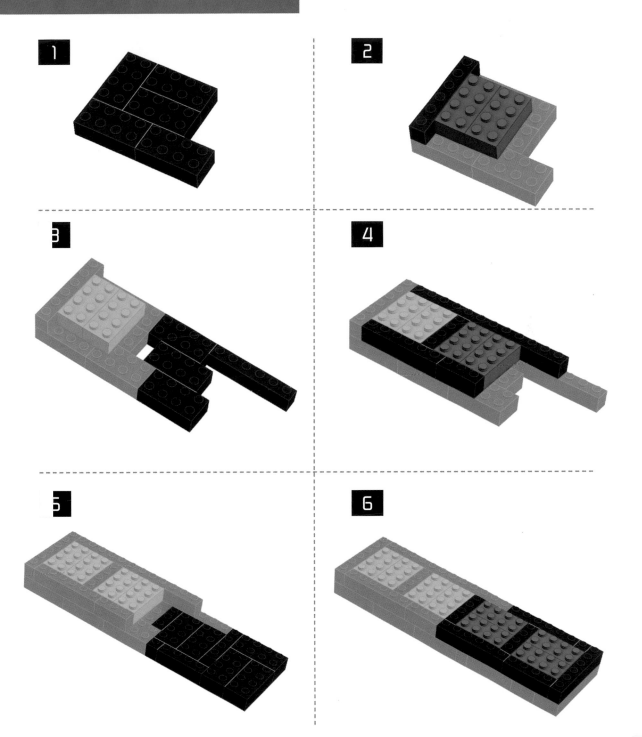

1

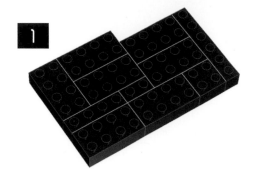

2

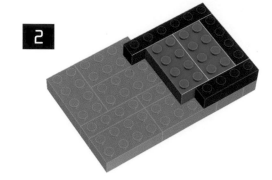

3

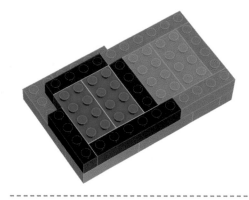

4

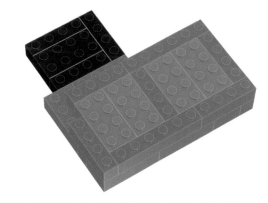

5

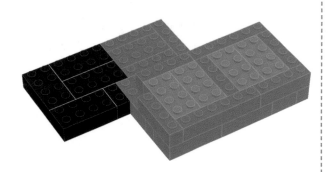

6

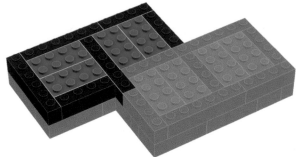

BLUE BRICKS

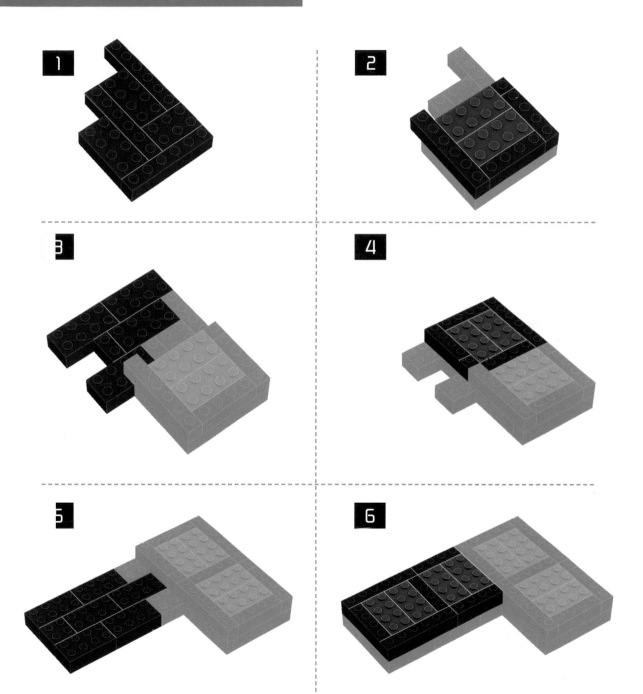

See page 128 for magnet instruction

BEAR-SKIN RUG

Impress your friends with your very own furry friend. Part trophy, part tray, why not bring a little grizzly to the table?

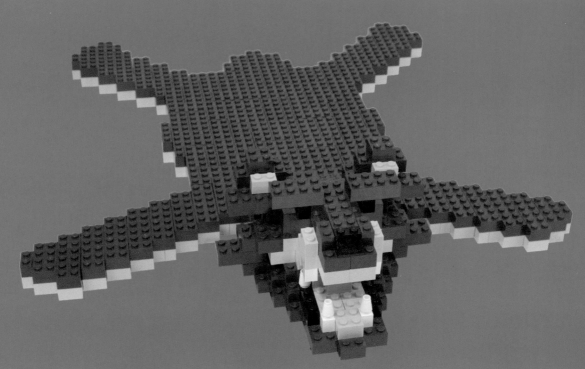

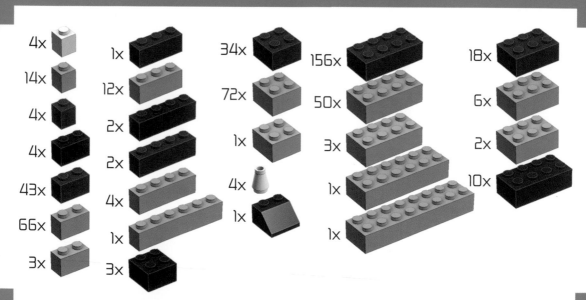

THE HEAD

1

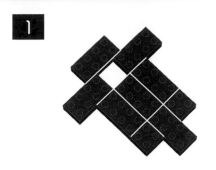

2

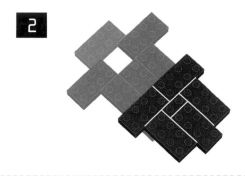

3

4

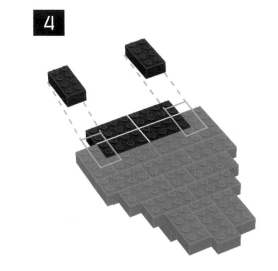

5

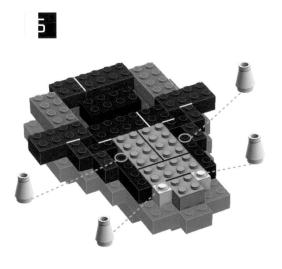

6

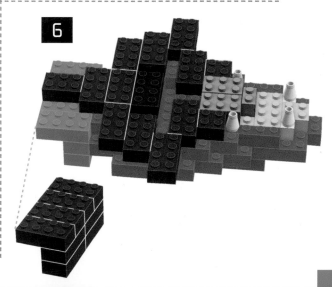

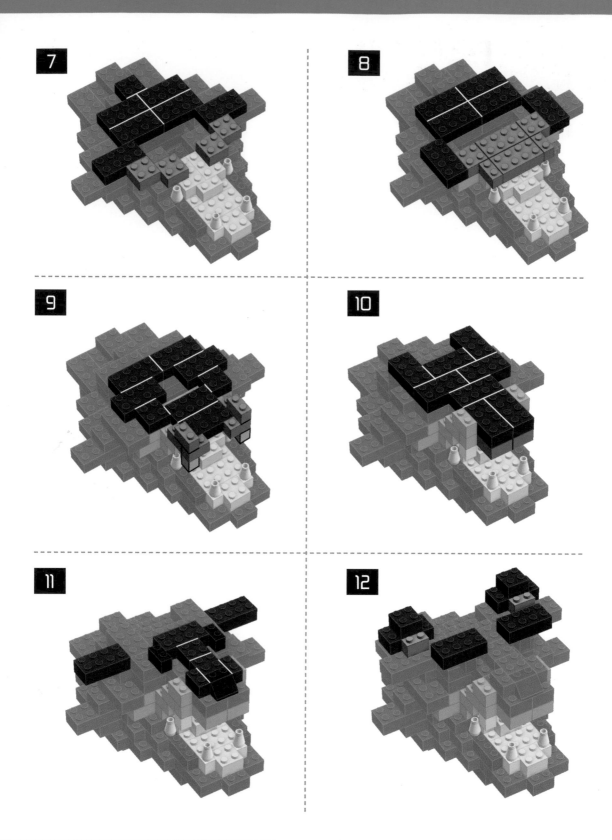

THE BODY

1

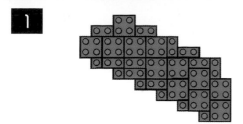

2

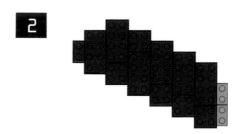

3

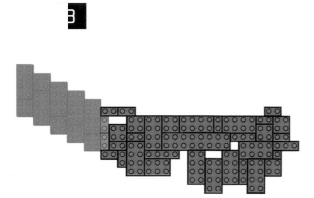

4

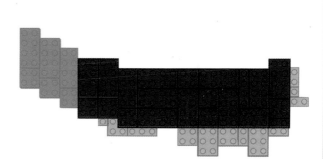

5

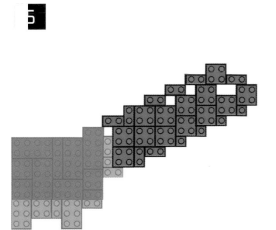

6

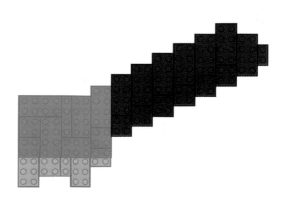

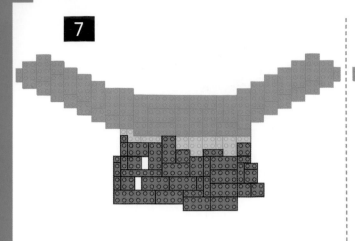

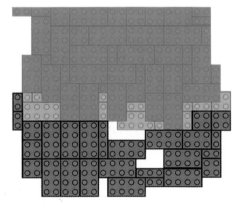

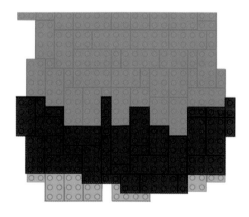

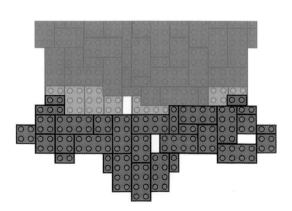

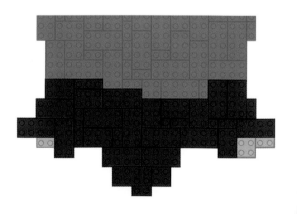

13

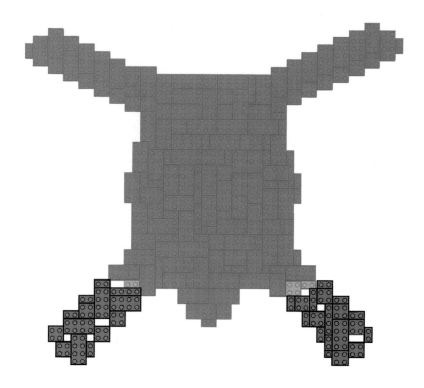

14

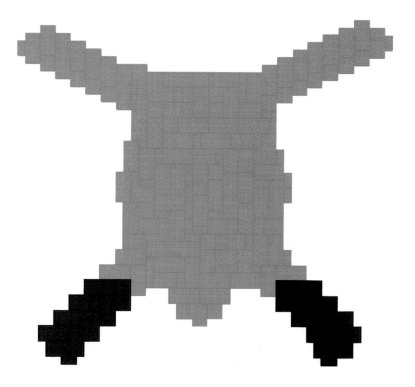

15

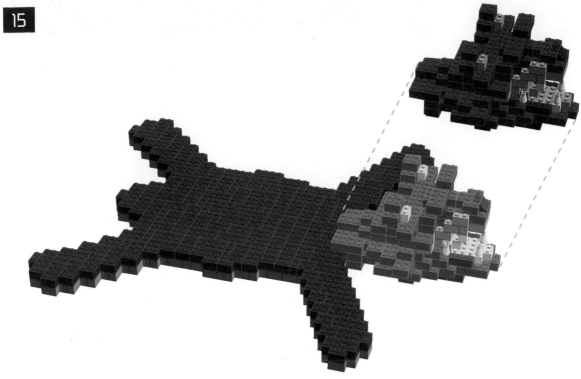

16

Stand back, she's gonna blow! A little tricky to construct, but well worth it when you have, this volatile vessel is sure to bring some bang to your flower display.

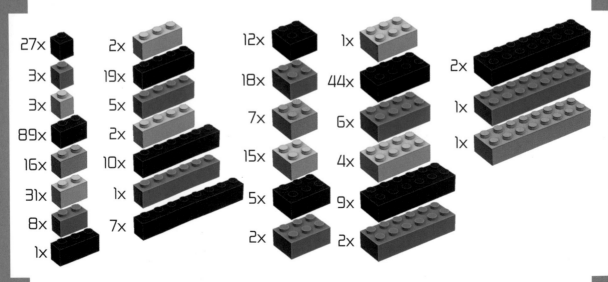

27x
3x
3x
89x
16x
31x
8x
1x

2x
19x
5x
2x
10x
1x
7x

12x
18x
7x
15x
5x
2x

1x
44x
6x
4x
9x
2x

2x
1x
1x

THE BODY

1

2

3

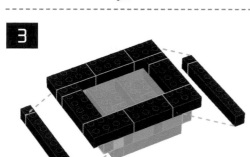

4

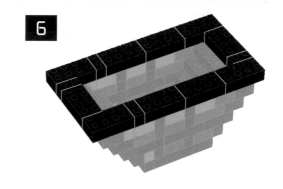

5

6

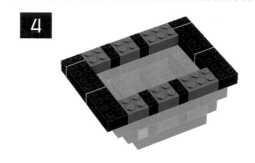

7

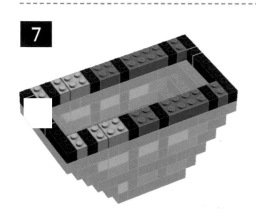

8

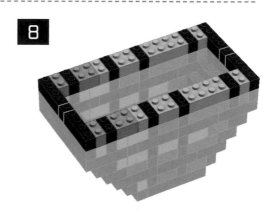

9

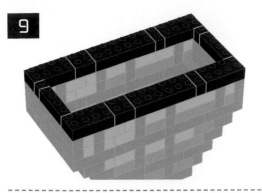

10

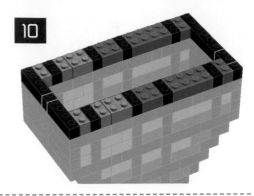

11

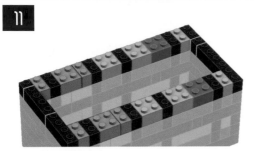

12

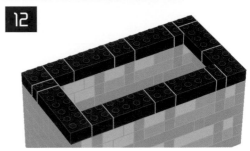

THE NECK

1

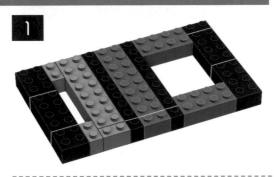

2

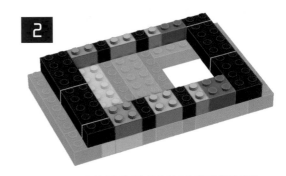

3

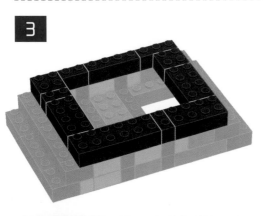

4

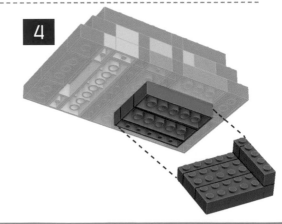

THE POT

1

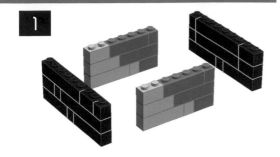

2

3

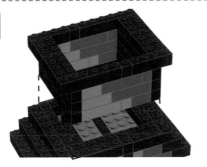

THE PIN

1

2

THE LEVER

1

2

3

These two 1980s androids are the perfect servants to hold your wine bottle. Fiercely loyal, the boozy bots don't move unless commanded to do so.

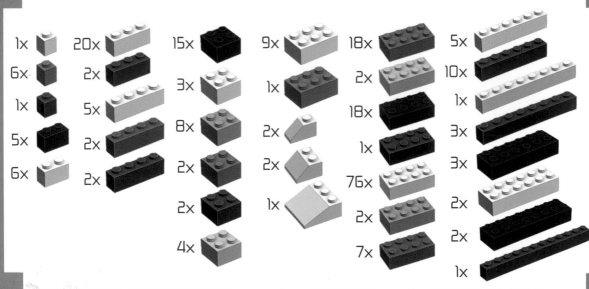

1x 20x 15x 9x 18x 5x

6x 2x 3x 2x 10x

1x 5x 8x 1x 18x 1x

5x 2x 2x 1x 3x

6x 2x 2x 2x 76x 3x

2x 2x 2x

4x 7x 2x

1x

SMALL ROBOT

1

2

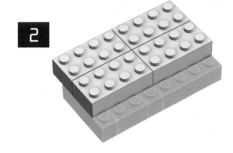

3

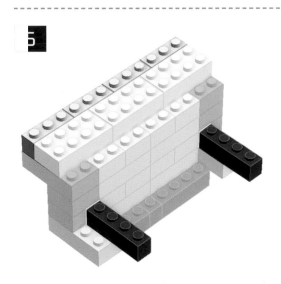

4

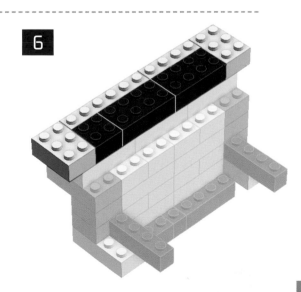

5

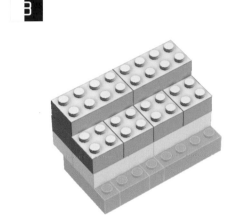

6

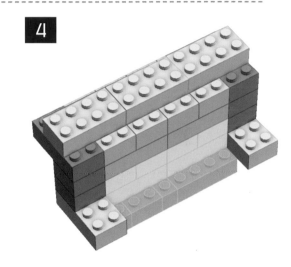

7

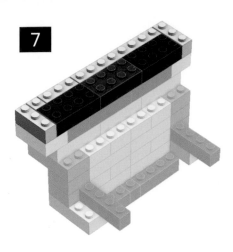

8

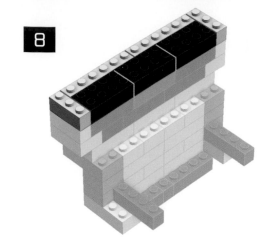

9

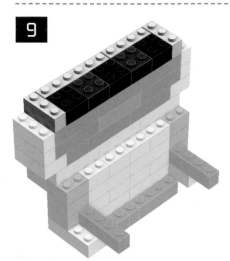

10

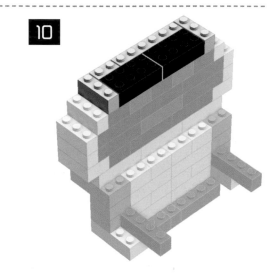

11

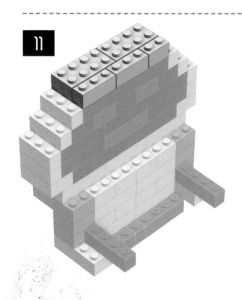

BIG ROBOT

1

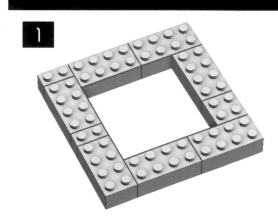

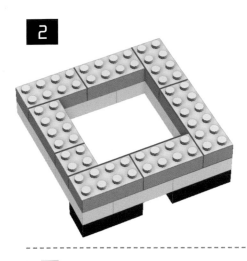

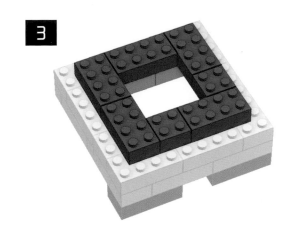

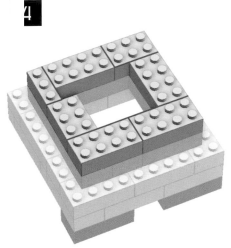

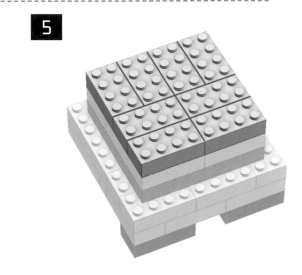

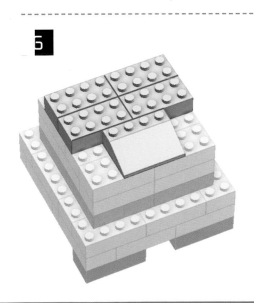

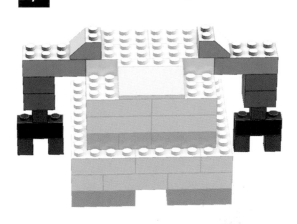

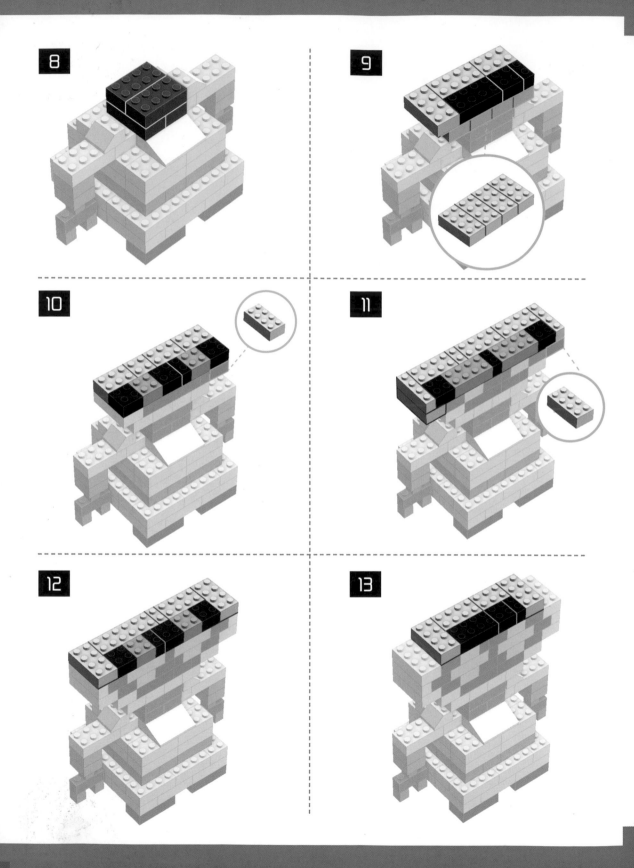

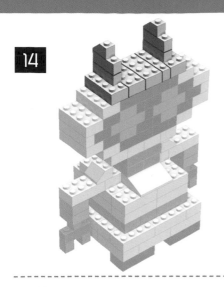

14

1

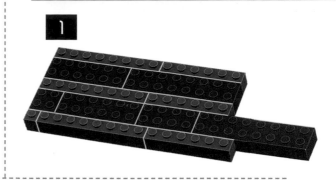

2

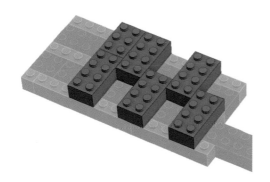

3

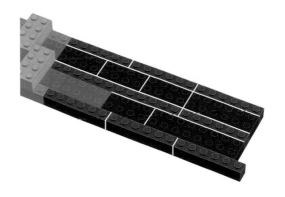

4

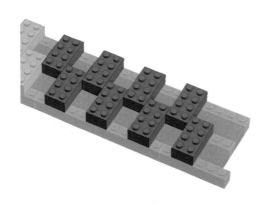

5

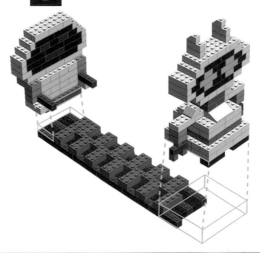